Quick n Dirty Marketing Tips

Find out what works and what doesn't... today

by Jason D C Sullock

Dedicated to Linda, Wendy & David, and Sharon
The people who keep me sane (allegedly)

Content

Introduction

Have you ever been told something and thought… "Why didn't I think of that?" Or, seen something, and said to yourself… "Ah I understand how it works now."

That's like Marketing. It's all commonsense, but it's only commonsense once you've been shown how it's done.

Once you know what to do and why to do it, you can create marketing that works every time.

This book will show you how... read on...

Why it pays to cut corners…

If I can identify the marketing techniques that work and don't work without going through all the trial and error, then I'm happy.

So here's the first secret:

1. Normal marketing processes don't usually change. Somebody's done it – or something similar – before.

   So ask yourself... do you want to spend the next twenty years of your life testing marketing that's been tested before?

   Or would you rather be stacking the cards in your favour, by using techniques that you already know will be successful?

   And no… it's not cheating. It's being smart. Anyone who suggests otherwise is wasting their own valuable time.

   If you'd rather be successful… then get reading.

What are the rules and can you break them?

I want to make you this promise. You can break all the rules…

…but first you need to learn what they are, so you know

a) What rules you're breaking.

b) Why you're going to break them.

Why is this so important? Here's the second secret:

2. If you break the rules without understanding why and you succeed… you're just lucky, and it's unlikely you'll be able to repeat the success, except under exactly the same circumstances (which rarely happen)

And if you break the rules and fail… you'll never understand why, and you won't know what to change to help you succeed the next time.

You break the rules when you clearly understand the risks and the opportunities.

Your approach…

3. Your approach to marketing is incredibly important. There is an acronym that is used in most large companies – PPPPP – Planning Prevents Piss Poor Performance. . It's one of those bullshit-bingo acronyms that people quote, but that many ignore.

   You ignore it at your peril. This chapter is about planning how you'll be successful.

4. Military commanders have a saying "No plan survives contact with the enemy." This applies to marketing as well.

5. When you are planning a marketing campaign, do what military commanders do to ensure their troops know what to do after the plan has gone out of the window; provide yourself with 'intent'.

6. 'Intent' is a guide to what you want to achieve overall. Why is this important? Because with it, you, your design agency, or your team, will always know what you need to do, even if you have to change the tactics.

7. Writing copy is like going on a date…

   a) You - Would you like to go to the pictures?
   b) Your reader - Do I know you or are you a stalker?
   c) You – So will you go out with me?
   d) Your reader - Are you worth my time?
   e) You – This is what I have to offer.
   f) Your reader – okay, I'll go to the pictures with you.

8. Use the Acronym S.U.C.C.E.S. to write your copy. S – Simplicity; U – Unexpected; C – Concrete; C-Credible; E – Emotional; S – Stories.

9. Simplicity – strip your product or service back to its basics. You need to give the customer a central reason to be interested.

10. Unexpected – Jar the customer out of their complacency. The human brain 'files' memories and learning's for easy access. It builds up these memories into a 'schema' for quick reference. For example, if I say 'a car' your mind could bring up the basic schema of, say… a Ford Focus, but if I say 'a red sports car' the chances are your mind will bring up the schema for a Ferrari. To capture Interest, you must first break the customer's schema that what you're showing them is just 'more of the same'.

    You break the customer's initial short-cut schema by pointing out something that is unusual, or by asking them a question they're not sure they know the answer to. This causes them to metaphorically 'sit up and take interest'. For example, a lecturer could start a session to students by saying "Global Warming is a fact!" which is complying with the student's schema, and then continue "Or is it?", which suddenly breaks the student's nice logical, memory driven filing system, and causing them to be more attentive.

    But capturing the customer interest is obviously not enough. You need to hold their interest until you have finished your pitch. How do you do that?

    You continue to hold the customer's attention by showing them that they have further gaps in their knowledge… gaps in their schemas.

    You then fill these 'knowledge gaps' with interesting facts and benefits from your product or service.

11. Concrete – This is usually where business communications go wrong. Mission statements and visions are usually ambiguous. You must fill your copy with everyday 'concrete' images that the customer can easily relate to. For example, the saying 'A bird in the hand is worth two in the bush' has been around for millennia. Why? Because you can relate to it. It's concrete. Most business people drive a car, so when you're describing an easy-to-see set of

software reports, a concrete word to use might be 'dashboard'.

12. Credible – Credibility is about being able to test what you've heard for yourself. So when you're talking to customers, offer them a means of 'checking you out independently'. This need not involve huge expense. For instance, you could ask them to ask themselves a question 'Before you look any further, ask yourself, would you have a better work/life balance if you could cut your paperwork down?'

    By giving your customer the ability to independently test you, you're building up the credibility of your offer.

13. Emotion – Human beings are hard-wired for emotions. We don't care about numbers, but we do care about causes and feelings. What feelings do you want your audience to have when they are reading your copy? Pride that they are part of an exclusive club? Smart, that they're shaving off three hours needless admin work by using your product?

14. Stories – Stories work! Veteran soldiers swap stories with rookies to teach them how to survive. Parents tell fables to their children to teach them right from wrong. You and I use quotations and sayings to illustrate by example what we mean. Hearing a story is like simulator training for your brain. You're setting up a basic schema ready to be filled with memories. If you tell your audience what to expect, then they'll expect it. For example, if you tell your audience 'this is what will happen when you sign up', then they will be mentally prepared for what will happen. But a warning… you must make happen what you say will happen, otherwise your credibility will be instantly lost.

15. Remember AIDCA (Awareness, Interest, Desire, Conviction, Action). These are the stages every buyer must go through in order to make a purchase. Sometimes a single stage might take months,

sometimes it can happen subconsciously within a second, but all must go through them.

16. Always set a goal. If you don't set a goal, how will you know if you've succeeded?

17. Always set a goal that is higher than what you're used to. That way you'll 'grow' each time.

18. Always know how you're going to measure your success.

19. There's no such thing as failure. There's success, and there are learning's. Do you think Thomas Edison invented the light bulb at the first attempt? Or do you think he created thousands of designs that provided him with increased knowledge each time?

20. If you or your bosses are looking for instant success, then stick with what works.

21. If you do what has worked, and you do it well, you are guaranteed – the situation being the same - to get similar results.

22. If you or your bosses want something different, you need to change the landscape. You need to break some of your rules, so you get a different result. It won't always succeed, and it takes time, so don't fool yourself.

23. Don't dream. Do. If you want it badly enough, you'll find a way.

24. Don't have regrets. You are you. Therefore the decisions you make are your decisions… the only ones you could make at the time. Don't beat yourself up for them. Learn from decisions you don't like.

25. Don't live other people's lives and opinions. Have your own.

26. Stand out from the crowd. I once watched ten thousand teenagers and students bouncing up and down in unison to the Green Day Song 'I want to be the Minority'. Did they stand out? Were they the minority?

27. Right and wrong is a matter of perspective. Some people hate The Angel of the North, some people love it. They're not right, they're not wrong, they just have an opinion. Creating good marketing is not about opinion, it's about facts. Stick to the facts.

Insights…

If only you could inhabit the mind of a customer for just five minutes, what insights would you gain? What advantages would you have in selling to them knowing their every move? This chapter will help you… read on.

28. You usually have 2 seconds to get a prospect's interest.

29. If you're talking to customer's you probably have a bit more… 5 seconds.

30. They are not interested in your products. They are interested in you solving their problems.

31. You need to solve their problems... so you need to know what their problems are, and how your product/service can solve them… so you need to listen to them first.

32. On Direct Mail – A letter will typically get you 75% of your orders; a brochure will account for a further 15%; and the order form will get you the remaining 10%.

33. One piece mailers are cheap… but they hardly ever beat envelope enclosed responses, except perhaps where the customer is not normally given to handling lots of envelopes… such as in an outside job role.

34. Learn from a flop, but don't try to tweak it better. If you do, you're just wasting your valuable time.

35. Be damned sure you are not embarrassed to own up to your marketing. If you are, you shouldn't have put it out there in the public domain in the first place.

36. Always test

37. Document all you're testing.

38. Good data can raise your response rate by a factor of six.

39. A good offer can raise your response rate by a factor of four.

40. Good creative can only raise your response rate by a factor of one point two.

41. When you're asking customers to call you, tell them you're busy. It has been proved that saying 'If advisors are busy, please call again' increases response. Why? Because people don't just want to make decisions, they want to be making the 'right' decisions. There is comfort in numbers. If a phone line is engaged, then there must be other people buying as well.

42. Providing examples of 'social proof', for example, that 'the majority of guests re-used their towels in this hotel' can significantly increase the response you get for a similar action. In this example, the increase was between 26% and 33%.

43. Don't use the testimonials you're most proud of, use the testimonials that are most comparable with your audience.

44. Avoid negative statements, for instance '36 patients did not show up for their appointments last month'. Whilst this might be true, it embeds in the reader's mind that 'not showing up' is the norm, rather than something to be ashamed of.

45. People have a natural tendency to do what most people do… so tell them what most people have done. Use Positive statements. For instance '700,000 people have already installed Sage software at the heart of their business.' This provides a positive role model, and again, there is comfort in the numbers who have already made the decision.

46. If your best customers are already doing what you want. Don't just ignore them… reaffirm that they're doing the right thing. It doesn't cost much, but try to make it visual… perhaps a tick and a thank you on their messaging. If you ignore them, they'll slide toward the norm, and usually the norm is less than your best.

47. Don't offer too many options. For two offers in a relevant pension fund, the take up was 75%, but this reduced by 2% for every ten option added. For sales of a Jam, six options can create a 30% take-up. Quadruple the number of choices to twenty-four and this reduces sales to 3%. A well known shampoo producer reduces its range from twenty-six to fifteen products, and gains 10% in sales. Analysis paralysis… the brain can't handle it… hence disengagement.

48. If you don't put a recommended value against a free gift, the 'worth' of that free gift will be reduced in the eyes of the customer by 35%.

49. This idea of giving a free gift 'worth' extends to time as well, e.g. an hour's consultation.

50. Customers tend to favour compromise choices, between the minimum they need, and the maximum they can afford.

51. Fear usually stimulates an audience to respond, but can paralyze decision where clear, effective calls to action are not included.

52. The norm of society drives customers toward returning favours in their business dealings. In one experiment a small free gift from a stranger produced twice as many sales at a later date, despite the seller deliberately not mentioning the earlier free gift. Even an 'offer' of something free at the beginning of a conversation – be it a gift, or to put in a good word with their boss – can have a significantly positive effect on the relationship at a later time… as long as you keep your promise.

53. Hand-written notes on post-it notes attached to mailers improve response rates by 35% when compared to mailers without them. Why? As above, people recognise the extra effort it takes to write a note, and return the favour.

54. Giving something 'extra' and making it seem that you have done it purely for that particular customer… almost as an afterthought for them being so good, can increase the will to pay more in the future by up to 23%.

55. Lead by example. If you state that you've made a donation to a charity on the customer's behalf, and then ask them to reciprocate the gesture by doing a non-profit making service, you will increase the likelihood of them doing so by 45%, when compared to simply asking them to make the gesture.

56. A 'foot-in-the-door' approach followed by a bigger request can increase the uptake of the second request by up to 31%, when compared to a single approach.

57. Labeling your customer with a positive trait or attitude does work. In tests, voters who were told that they were 'good citizens' after completing a survey, were 15% more likely to vote a week later.

58. You can increase the likelihood of a customer responding by up to 20%, simply by asking them if they are going to respond beforehand. As long as the action is seen as being positive and something the customer 'should' do, when it comes to responding, they are more likely to.

59. Be consistent in what you ask your audience to do. The older the audience, the more consistent in your behaviour they will want you to be.

60. Giving your audience praise for consistently choosing your product helps ensure they will do so again.

61. Asking for a little helps response a lot. It tests for charities the phrase 'even a penny will help' increased response rates by 21.4%.

62. In the above tests, the responders also gave 63% more in donations.

63. Do readers disbelieve testimonials? Let's face it; companies are hardly going to say their products or services are rubbish, are they? But in fact, tests show that a third party 'believer', who speaks to your customer about you, makes you more trustworthy. Why? Because it's not you who is boasting.

64. By touting your weakness, you can improve your trustworthiness, and ensure that when you talk about your positives, you're more readily believed.

65. If you link your weaknesses to benefits, you will also be seen as more trustworthy. For example: We can only take up to ten trainees on each course, but that means you'll get more one-to-one time with the trainer.

66. If you make a mistake, own up to it. Research shows that companies that own up have a higher share price one year later, than those that blame external factors.

67. Those who receive a mailing from someone who has a similar name to themselves, is nearly twice as likely to respond - 56% compared to 30%.

68. A disproportionate number of customers – usually between 70-80% in the USA – have a job that can be associated with the same letter as their first name. Why can this be important? Well, if you were going to approach Construction companies, you might get a better response by signing the letter from 'Christopher'.

69. If you're in sales, one of the best things you can do to increase the customers confidence in you, is repeat back what they're looking for. This positive

confirmation that you have heard the customer correctly, clinches deals in 67% of the time, compared to a paltry 12.5% for those simply acknowledging the customer.

70. Scarcity improves sales. By placing a limited on your time, products, or services, you are imbuing them with value… a value that might have been unappreciated in the past. In one test, simply acknowledging that business knowledge came from 'an exclusive source' increased requests for the information by 600%.

71. Customers have a tendency to be more sensitive to loss than to gain. Removing something they have used for a long period of time causes consternation, unless there is a clear and positive instruction on how to continue.

72. As a follow-up to the above. If you can get your customers to describe why they like doing business with you… 'because you are…', they are far more likely to end up praising you.

73. If you ask your customer to name ten benefits of using your products, you're more likely to turn them off you than if you asked them to name one benefit. Why? Failing to know ten benefits shows that your product can't be 'that good' because 'I don't know much about it', whereas knowing one major benefit is a success… and people like being successful.

74. A simple to pronounce product name will always be more affectionately thought of than an unpronounceable one. The more affectionately thought of… yes, you guessed it; the more likely people are to buy.

75. Rhyming slogans are more easily processed by customers than non-rhyming. Tests show that rhymes are thought to be more accurate.

76. Perceptual contrast. No, it's not something Philosophers discuss, and it can really help in marketing situations. If you give the customer a 'little information' on a product, followed by 'lot of information' for a second product, the customer will feel disproportionably knowledgeable about the second. The customer is 'unwittingly' comparing what they have read and making a judgement that they understand the second message far better.

77. If you're running a loyalty programme, or a 'collect the vouchers to get the discount' campaign, if you give the customer or prospect a head start on the collection (i.e.: you give them two vouchers to get them going), not only will more customers start collecting, but they'll do it faster, than those who just get a blank collection card.

78. Giving something commonplace an additional name – for instance 'Frosty Orange' – adds an air of mystery to it, and this increases Interest in the item. Of course, you must then explain why it's called 'Frosty Orange' to maintain the customer's interest.

79. Marketers often use branding to increase the awareness of their business, but failure to carry through the branding to their packaging can result in great memorable campaigns, with absolutely no uplift in sales. Brand marketers can assume that the customer will naturally remember the company name in the advert. This can be naïve – and the best in the world have made this mistake – so always ensure you make the connection between the advert and the packaging in the retail environment.

80. Mirrors are a powerful reminder of the need to behave according to social norms. In tests, placing a mirror beside objects can reduce theft of that object by up to 24.8%. What's this got to do with marketing? Wherever you are asking the customer or prospect to examine their behaviour… for instance, in a charity campaign, the use of a mirror like element, or perhaps even the drawing of a mirror with the type

of behaviour your require in it, might increase your response.

81. Be unexpected when naming. Weird as it seems, people are much more likely to buy 'halfcakes' than 'cupcakes' at a fete; and they're much more likely to buy something low-cost from a door-to-door salesman if they are told the price in pennies.

82. To reach a 'tipping point' in spreading a virus, you need three things: 1) a network for spreading the virus, 2) a carrier of the virus, and 3) a sticky virus message.

83. In marketing terms, a viral message spreads via a number of channels to market, usually social media like face book, Twitter, or LinkedIn, gaining momentum as it contacts more and more people who pass the virus on.

84. A carrier is someone who becomes an advocate of the message, and who actively spreads the virus. Not everyone is an advocate. Not everyone will become a carrier. An epidemic will only occur when enough carriers have been found within the network.

85. A sticky virus message will aid the start of an epidemic. If the virus message is too limited, by timescales or size of audience for instance, the epidemic will not have enough scope to take hold and be passed on in its turn.

86. A sales funnel can typically be divided into four sections:

    - Thought Leadership and Problems solving
    - Core Products & Services
    - Specific Offers
    - Sales Pipeline

    The further down the sales funnel you drive them, the less leads you will get, but the faster those leads will convert into sales.

Conversely, the higher up the sales funnel you catch them the more leads you'll get, but the longer it will take you to convert them to sales.

But your best options for quick revenue always lie in the Sales Pipeline.

The Sales Pipeline is the home of all those lovely leads that you have so carefully driven inbound to your sales team and that your sales team hasn't converted yet. They've languished there, and will continue to cool until they've gone completely cold… unless you keep them warm and make them offers.

87. Some people call them 'freebies', others call them 'teasers', I call them bait pieces.

Bait pieces are things that you give away to your audience to try to engage them and get them talking to you on a subject.

In other words they're 'bait', as in fishing.

There are many different types of bait…

Salmon fishermen use rods and fish in rivers… deep sea fishermen use trawlers and huge nets in the North Sea… my grandfather used to use grenades in small Iraqi lakes between the wars.

My point is that you wouldn't think of going to fish for Salmon in a lake. You wouldn't take grenades to go fishing in the North Sea. You wouldn't use a Trawler net on a small Salmon river in Scotland.

It's the same when you're choosing bait pieces to engage an audience. Choose the most appropriate pieces for the audience.

88. Churchill once said that the winners of World War II would be the side that made the least mistakes. He

recognised that he would make mistakes. His aim was to make as few as he could.

89. In the darkest days of World War II, when France had fallen and the Invasion of Britain was thought to be imminent, and Churchill was asked what he intended to do, he said that he would 'KBO' – Keep Buggering On.

90. There are two different types of marketing people – a) Those that want to get it perfect, and then launch, b) those that want to launch, and then make alterations as they go. The two don't mix.

91. The invention of the Internet has led to a phenomenon called the 'Long Tail'. This simply means that somewhere in the world will be someone who wants what you have to sell, and that you stand a much better chance of finding them now because they don't have to walk into your bricks-and-mortar shop to buy it.

92. The Internet has greatly increased the ability of customers to communicate to each other without using traditional hierarchical structures – i.e.: they don't need to go through middlemen. This has caused, and is causing, huge problems for existing institutions and leaders. How do you lead when the followers you thought you had don't need to go through you anymore?

93. Think about this for a second or two. This is epoch shattering. It's like Martin Luther starting the Religious Reformation by saying that you don't need a priest to talk to God any more. How do you think the Catholic Church viewed that?

Like everything, this idea has both positive and negative aspects.

Imagine a big empty square in a city. Over the day it slowly fills up. People start to wander around. They start talking to each other. All are equals. All have an opinion. Some might get on well with many other people in the city square. Others might want to stick to the people close to them.

Then a man comes into the square. He sets up a box, climbs up, and starts talking.

The other people turn to listen. Some like what the speaker is saying and they gravitate toward him. Some people listen for a few seconds and then turn back to their friends.

The area around the speaker starts to contain people with common interests. When the listeners talk to each other they find they have goals and views in common. They agree with each other.

The speaker has brought them together and introduced them. That speaker has become their new leader.

But he's not a 'do as I say' leader. That's 'Old World' thinking. This leader is a facilitator. He still has power, but it's the power of suggestion, and the power of introduction to other people. In the language of Malcolm Gladwell's book 'The Tipping Point' they are a Connector.

94. The Internet has provided the tools to do this – to bypass existing systems. You need to provide the suggestions and the new leadership.

95. Be decisive in your work. You might not always be right, but you'll be respected.

96. If you're having a problem, it's probably because you're playing by someone else's rules. Don't.

97. It's easier to beg forgiveness than to ask permission… but be damned sure you're going to succeed before you do it. Commit to whatever it is you're going to do wholeheartedly.

98. If you don't make it happen, no-one will make it happen for you.

99. If you can't deliver it, don't promise it.

100. Don't try to be infallible. You're not. Get used to it.

Writing copy…

Anybody can write copy, right? Yes… but the trick is to write good copy, and good copy takes thought, and knowledge, and planning, and an understanding of previous results. Everything in this chapter will help you short-cut years of trial and error.

Read on…

101. Say what you need to say, in as few words as possible.

102. Start with what you know – the calls to action (telephone numbers etc.) – then move on to what you want the reader to do (i.e.: call 0800… and speak to…), and what they can expect when they've done it (i.e.: We will send you… within… days; you can then download…).

103. Be absolutely clear on what you're saying.

104. Not knowing what to do, and not knowing what will happen next, is a major contribution to non-response.

105. Write the core of the Direct Mail only after you have done this. Knowing the space you have left is helpful in 'filling the gaps' with copy.

106. Write the first draft quickly, put it aside, then go back to it and edit. The real crux of the copy will usually be found in the second or third paragraph of the copy.

107. Unless you have a complete brain-wave, write the headline last. That way your mind has already digested what you want the reader to do, how they should do it and why they should be interested.

108. The shorter the line width, the more readability you get.

109. Ensure your first line is as short as possible to draw the reader into the copy.

110. You will meet people who are grammar fanatics. Let me tell you now, I am not. Why? Very simply, the objective of writing copy is not 'to be grammatically correct'; it is 'to sell'. So you do whatever it takes 'to sell'. If this happens to be grammatically correct, then great. If not, don't worry.

111. Use connectors. Connectors are anything that makes the reader carries on reading. Examples of connectors are …, and, but, next, so, numbered items, arrows, etc.

112. Want to keep them reading past the first page? Tell them. By putting 'read on…' or 'more overleaf…' or 'continued…' at the bottom right of the page, your audience will do as you ask.

113. Use simple everyday language – i.e.: 'Lift' instead of 'elevator', 'motorway' instead of 'major trans-national trade network'.

114. Always ask yourself 'will this make sense to my customer?'

115. Use of the word 'free' in your headline will increase response rate.

116. Use of the word 'new' in your headline will increase response rate.

117. Telling the reader what you want them to do (i.e.: Call, download, complete the form) will increase response rate.

118. Don't cry 'Wolf'. In other words, don't say things like 'hurry – sale ending soon' if it's due to end in two months time.

119. How much you tell the reader depends on whether you have a sales team or online store, or whether you have to sell 'off the page'.

120. In general, the fewer sales resources you have, the more you have to do a thorough job of selling off the page.

121. Pepper your copy with Google Adwords that you are bidding on. That way if the reader is looking for extra information on the web, they're more likely to choose the exact words you've used and won at auction.

122. Add a signature if possible. Signatures work in the same way as post-it notes. They show that someone has taken the time to add an extra touch to the mailing.

123. If you are going to use a competition, by law you must include Terms & Conditions. These 'T&C's' don't have to be on your piece of marketing itself – you can get away with 'Terms &Conditions apply – please see www.tc.co.uk' to save space.

124. Thirty headline shortcuts to use in a hurry:

- Begin with 'introducing'
- Begin with 'Announcing'
- Use words that seem like an announcement
- Begin with 'New'
- Begin with 'Now'
- Begin with 'At last'
- Use a date in your headline
- Write your headline in the style of a newspaper article
- Use a 'reduced price' in your headline
- Use a 'special offer' in your headline
- Use an 'Easy-payment' plan in your headline
- Use a 'free' offer
- Offer 'valuable information'
- Tell a story

- Begin with 'How to'
- Begin with 'Why'
- Begin with 'Which'
- Begin with 'Who else?'
- Begin with 'Wanted'
- Begin with 'This'
- Begin with 'Because'
- Begin with 'If'
- Begin with 'Advice'
- Use a testimonial
- Use a one word headline
- Use a two word headline
- Use a three word headline
- Warn the reader to delay until they've read your copy
- Ask a question
- Offer easily relatable facts

125. Fourteen effective appeals

- Make money
- Save money
- Money security
- Health security
- Better health now
- Old age security
- Professional advancement
- Respect
- Enjoyment
- Make your work easier
- Have more leisure time
- Live in comfort
- Become thin
- Stop worrying

126. If you're looking for effective appeals you could do a lot worse than remember the seven deadly sins – but of course, you need to use the 'lite' version of them.

127. To be a good copywriter, you must be a good psychologist. Put yourself in the position of Sherlock Holmes, or Cracker. Copywriting is just applied psychology.

128. Before you begin your writing, imagine yourself shepherding the customer down a long corridor with doors along either side. You want to the customer to exit using the last door at the bottom of the hall.

129. The trouble is that all the other doors have nice, easy, simple and enticing reasons for the customer to avoid doing what you want… too expensive; too complex; too hard to learn; etc.

130. You must metaphorically 'shut and lock each door' before you can shepherd the customer down the hall and out the exit you need them to go through.

131. Successful responses are more likely if you use a headline with a strong and specific appeal in them.

132. Specific appeal headlines generate three times as many responses as general appeal headlines.

133. Don't tell your customer they are important whilst addressing them as 'Mr. A. Fish'. This simply exposes your inadequate data, and ultimately your level of interest in being authentic with the customer.

134. Find something in your offer you believe in. That way, when you're selling the offer, you'll be much more authentic in your tone.

135. Don't try to change your customer's behaviour. Work with them and change your process to suit them.

136. Always, always, remember that human beings have not changed mentally in over 100,000 years… so assume that your customer has the same level of smarts as you.

137. Trust me… if a customer can misunderstand your copy… they will.

138. If someone you work with and who knows what you're trying to sell, can't read your copy out loud without stumbling, then rewrite it.

139. If a customer doesn't want to do it, they won't do it. You need to get them to want to do it.

140. Don't forget to add Terms & Conditions to an offer if you need to.

141. Always run Terms & Conditions past a legal expert before you go live.

142. Be specific. Specifics sell. General points don't. Get to the point quickly.

143. Personalise if possible… especially on the letter/DM and on an order form.

144. Handwritten messages always get noticed, as long as they are handwritten, and not typeset printed.

145. Break up large areas of text into smaller, more manageable ones.

146. Try not to repeat the same copy on different parts of your marketing. Customer's, who need an excuse to stop reading, will stop reading because of it.

147. Tables and graphs grab attention.

148. Setting a line at an angle grabs attention.

149. Never justify your text. It makes the eye pass quickly over it.

150. In an analysis of over 250 DM pieces that were used for more than three consecutive years, and were therefore successful, the majority of them appealed to either greed or flattery.

151. Twelve powerful words:

- You
- Save
- Money
- Easy
- Guarantee
- Health
- Results
- New
- Love
- Discovery
- Proven
- Safety

152. Wherever possible, use the first person – 'you' and 'me' – people buy from people, not from faceless companies.

153. Always make it easier to say 'yes' than to say 'no'.

154. Prospects buy dreams… sell them the dream.

155. Be clear, be brief, keep the reader moving… but if you need a thousand words to get the message across, don't be afraid of taking it.

156. Everything is interesting… even, God forbid… Coleslaw, you just have to understand why and to whom.

157. Negativity repels… positivity attracts.

158. Hit deadlines. Salespeople want regularity, not superb copy. Their sales depend on the marketing machine churning out leads for them.

159. Copywriting isn't about writing… it's about selling.

160. Never, ever, pad out your copy. The more copy there is, the easier it is to switch off as a reader.

161. Never, ever, start writing with product or service questions still buzzing around your head.

162. Wherever possible, use guarantees.

163. Always try to give more than the reader expects.

164. Keep in mind your readers budget when writing copy.

165. Keep in mind the limits on your reader's time.

166. Thank your reader early on in your copy.

167. Reward your readers again and again, as they read your copy.

168. Never go out (unless you absolutely have to) with first draft copy. It - nearly always – could be made even better by a good editing.

169. Build your headline around a major benefit.

170. Back up your benefit claims with case study proof. Customers regularly say they don't believe case studies, but in research, the offers with case studies always come out on top. What does that tell you?

171. Preview the offer as soon as possible, and then major on it further into the marketing.

172. When they have the good guy trapped, villains in films always start to brag about themselves. This inevitably gives the good guy the opportunity to escape…

173. Don't make their mistake. When you have the customer's attention, talk about their problems, their solutions. Don't start bragging about your company.

174. Don't use closed questions – questions that you can answer yes or no to – in your headline.

175. Kill – stone dead – any sexism or racism in your copy.

176. Check your copy out with at least three, and preferably five different types of reader. Do they all understand your copy?

177. Is your copy warm and personal to read? Or is it too cold and formal?

178. Does your copy 'look' exciting? Does it have underlines, headings, sub-headings, bullets, numbers, bold type?

179. Begin with your strongest selling point.

180. Make sure every picture has a caption.

181. Make sure your copy flows from one point to the next, and so on. There's nothing more off-putting to a reader than a disjointed…

182. Ensure that you are quite clear what your primary objective is and stick to it like glue. Don't let multiple objectives dilute your message.

183. Always be honest in your copy.

184. Putting quotes around a phrase helps customers accept the novelty of that phrase. It says to them that, we too, recognise that it's new, but that they and we shouldn't be afraid of it.

185. The further away from real life a number you use is – for example – 500 billion Sheep – the less it means to a reader. It's just too incomprehensible compared to say… three Sheep.

186. Brackets help you downplay something. (They tell the reader that what's in them is less important that what's before them.)

187. Only use exclamation points if you honestly believe what you are talking about is worth exclaiming!

188. The more a number departs from a rounded-off number, the more credible it seems to the reader. It sounds less made-up.

189. A 'dash (-)' is a hard transition. A 'dot dot dot (…)' is a soft transition. Use them wisely.

190. 'It' is a really weak word to begin a selling message with… except where you use it to flag a coming revelation, i.e.: "It was Sir Frank Whittle who invented the jet engine, and that…" In these cases, 'it' adds an air of 'historical conviction'… in other words, 'it's happened… it's a fact'.

191. 'The' is stronger than 'A' because The suggests that whatever you are talking about stands alone, as opposed to one of many.

192. Adding 'Will you?' at the end of a statement turns the hard statement into a warmer request.

193. 'When' suggests something will definitely happen. 'If' only suggests something might happen.

194. Always have a reason for using a headline, never a feeling.

195. Always determine the best appeal based on analysis, not hearsay or 'gut feel' wherever possible.

196. How to begin your body copy. Five lessons to use:

- Interrupt the reader's schema (see point 10)
- News style
- Preview summary of the main article
- Begin with a quotation
- Begin as a story

197. Why do Reader's Digest openings work? Things to notice:

- They're always full of facts

- They are easy to follow
- They are very specific
- They have few adjectives
- They arouse curiosity

198. Eleven recommended types of copy.

- Straightforward
- A story
- Speak directly to the reader – 'You and me' copy
- 'Imagine what it would be like' copy
- Factual copy
- Copy 'in the style of…'
- Truthful 'we do have faults' copy
- 'Blow your own trumpet' copy
- Signed guarantee copy
- 'I'm going to tease you again and again' copy
- Competitor comparison copy

199. Three types of copy to avoid at all costs.

- Poetic
- Extravagant
- Unbelievable

200. Eighteen ways to increase response.

- Use present tense
- Use subheads to break up monotonous copy
- Use captions under illustrations
- Use simple sentences
- Use simple words
- Give free information away
- Make sure all your sentences sell something
- Increase curiosity
- Make all your sentences specific as opposed to general
- Make sure that in your AIDCA process you give all the facts, no matter where you put them

- Always write more copy than you need… you can always edit down to the best and most appropriate copy
- Always ask for a response
- Be realistic in your statements
- Avoid cliché's
- Get other people to read your copy
- Don't tell the reader a sales person will call… it cuts down your response rates by 75%
- Make every campaign a complete AIDCA process
- Urge the reader to act now. Give them a reason to do so

201. Twenty-four ways to get more enquiries.

- Mention the offer!
- Highlight the word 'free'
- Mention the offer in the sub-headline
- Show a picture of whatever you're giving away for free
- Mention the offer in the first paragraph
- Use an interesting title for your give-away
- Give an attractive description of your give-away… sell your give-away
- If your give-away has anything to do with a famous person, highlight their name
- Include testimonials
- Sweeten your offer with a bonus
- Include a coupon
- Print a value on your give-away
- Include selling copy in your process for getting your give-away
- Make sure you have at least two instances of your telephone number
- Highlight any Calls to Action
- Highlight that there is 'no obligation' when ordering your give-away
- Highlight security when ordering sensitive information

- Urge immediate action
- Include Freephone or Freepost or free response Calls to Action
- Use a free-standing insert
- Offer several different offers
- Only contact your audience at the best time of year/month/day
- Copy the best selling ideas of your competitors

202. If you know your website will be prominently listed, be blatant about asking the reader to use your Google Adwords.

203. Don't use too many contractions (shan't instead of shall not)… it tires the eye and reduces readability.

204. Avoid difficult to read sentences… read them out loud. If you can't read them, and you wrote them, no-one else will be able to.

205. Avoid words that need explaining.

206. Offer proof that you're telling the truth.

207. Edit, edit, edit. Less is more… as long as you say what you need to say and show a complete AIDCA process.

208. Ask for the response… you cannot have too many Calls to Action (CTA's) in a Direct Mail…

209. …with one exception, don't have more than three to four CTA's all in one place.

210. The human brain is attuned to dealing with three-five choices at any one time. The more choices give the reader above this, the more 'analysis paralysis' you get.

211. That's not to say that you can't have more choices than this in any piece of creative, but just try to segment the choices into product or service groups, and have several different groupings.

212. Don't use jokes… don't be smart… everyone remembers your wit, not your product.

213. K.I.S.S. – Keep It Simple Stupid. Keep your message to one or two key points, and minimise the steps the reader has to take to respond.

214. The word 'because' can improve your chances of persuasion by up to 34%. For example 'Can I jump the queue because I'm running a bit late'; 'This widget will help you save time because it speeds up your systems'.

215. Get them to click through or go to your website. You can track it.

216. Give them a code to quote to sales people or put into your online store. You can track it.

217. Get them to call a dedicated telephone number for each offer. You can track it.

218. Get them to download something. You can track it.

219. Get them to trial something. You can track it.

220. Get them to take part in a forum. You can track it.

221. Get them to follow you on Twitter or Facebook. You can track it.

222. Get them to order or sign up for something online. You can track it.

223. If you can't track it, don't do it.

224. Text web links work much better than web adverts.

225. "Say what you need to say, in as few words as possible."

226. The whole point of copywriting is to drive responses into the sales funnel. How far down the sales funnel you drive them depends upon a number of factors:

- How much the customer knows about your company
- How much the customer knows about what you do
- How much the customer knows about the product or service you are promoting
- What stage the customer is at in the AIDCA process

227. For God's sake… ask for the sale!

228. Launches are combinations of both events and direct marketing. You need to understand both to make them work.

229. Always use checklists for launches, and always plan well in advance. Doing a launch 'on the fly' is just asking for trouble.

230. Web advertising was a fashion. In my opinion it doesn't work – especially in B2B – because your reader is just too switched on. You're better off sponsoring web links or providing editorial.

231. Trade press is dead. It just doesn't know it yet. As the next generation of Internet savvy readers joins the economy, there'll be a shift away from trade press. It's too expensive to produce, too expensive to deliver, too hard to track, and too hard to make agile changes.

232. Q&A forums, where you provide the experts and invite your audience to participate work brilliantly for encouraging engagement.

233. Twitter is brilliant for harnessing immediate change and disseminating important information. It provides you with the tools to harness crowds and turn them into your own evangelical tribe.

234. Keep an eye on developments for mobile advertising, even if you're in Business to Business. More and more people are using web application mobiles, and this allows them to access the Internet and have a real-time one-to-one digital engagement with you.

235. Unless you can tie the entry of a competition into a sales call or a concrete lead, all you'll get are 'freebie hunters' entering. You'll spend valuable resources chasing people who are never going to be interested in you or your products or services. It's better to get half the number of entries, and be certain that they're really interested in what you have to offer.

Design…

What do you want to get out of design? Do you want awards? If you do, leave design in the hands of the designers.

236. Do you want responses? Then tell your reader what to do - read on…

237. Messy interests the eye… alignment reduces response.

238. White on black, except in headlines, reduces readability.

239. Coloured text on white reduces readability.

240. The eye, in Western Europe and European descended/educated populations, reads top left to bottom right.

241. If you're using a main picture, ensure your headline is below it. A headline above a picture ensures that the reader's eye will go straight to the image, reducing message understanding.

242. If you are using a secondary picture, put a sub-headline with a benefit below it… why waste catching someone's eye by not highlighting something.

243. Try to make every component of your marketing campaign look (or sound) different. Difference attracts… regularity sucks.

244. The Keyhole views – many people only slit open the envelope and peek inside; many people only look at the preview of an email. Make sure your keyhole view has punch.

245. Hide part of your headline… ah, the curiosity factor!

246. Make each section look noticeably different.

247. The eye normally travels from dark areas to light areas.

248. Warm colours promote a warm response. Blue colours suggest science. Purple gets you extra revenue because of its regal associations.

249. Some pictures that attract attention well.

- Brides
- Babies
- Animals
- Famous people
- Odd costumes
- Odd situations
- Pictures that tell a story
- Romantic pictures
- Accidents and catastrophes
- News pictures
- Seasonal pictures

250. Some pictures that sell.

- Pictures of the product
- The product in use or the product providing a reward
- Achieving an ambition
- Enlarged detail from a product (as long as you have already show the full product and you can plainly see where the detail comes from)
- Dramatic pictures

251. A creative 'entry point' is something – an image, odd words, odd text, colours, shapes, etc. – that stops the readers eye when they're looking at your creative.

252. Good creative usually has several 'entry-points' for the eye.

253. A 'call out box', or 'call out', is a note attached to a main image that provides added information about the image.

254. Use call-out boxes to increase entry-points, and increase interest in your creative.

255. Dotted lines suggest coupons, and coupons suggest offers, and offers suggest bargains, and bargains tell the brain to 'read this'.

256. Repeat the offer on the coupon.

257. People looking out of the page attract the eye.

258. But only use people looking out of the page if you have a relevant reason for doing so. If you don't have a relevant reason, don't do it, you'll just frustrate people… "Why is she there?"

259. There's a difference between an Art Worker and a Designer. A Designer works on concepts… an Art Worker creates the final artwork.

260. Digital printing will allow you to personalise your marketing, but is only useful for print runs of up to 8,000-10,000.

261. You can never have enough personalization in your marketing. Readers love to see their name in print, even when they say it doesn't make a difference.

262. There is more than one type of paper you know. Some have a cheap feel, some look very expensive, some are plastic paper and can be opaque or even see-through… experiment, and record the results.

263. You can have shapes cut into mailings. You can create tabs that can be pulled like a pop-up book. You can create fold-out sections, or complicated origami shapes… experiment, and record the results.

264. You can add pop-up items to mailings. You can use boxes within boxes. You can even send pre-programmed USB cards that take the user straight to your website, or a cheap mobile phone that directly links them to your offices… experiment, and record the results.

265. The more cuts, folds, and gimmicks you use, the greater the cost of creation and fulfillment.

266. The heavier the item you design and create, the more it costs to mail.

267. If you are mailing, make sure the item fits through a letterbox!

268. There is CMYK printing – where the colours are made up of Cyan (Blue), Magenta (Red), Yellow, and Kino (Black) – and then there's RGB colours for PC's – Red, Green, Blue – and then there are Spot colours – Silver, Gold, Fluorescent, etc.

269. CMYK colour print with additional Spot colours can get very expensive, very quickly.

270. Always make sure you've added the Terms & Conditions to your artwork where you've used an offer. Failing this, you need to tell the reader where to find the Terms & Conditions on your website.

271. Steal from inspiration, but always remember to credit the originator. I stole this point from Paul Arden.

Events...

272. If you are organising a small local event, like a business breakfast, allow six weeks.

273. If you are organising a medium local event, like a business breakfast, allow eight to twelve weeks.

274. If you are organising a regional event, allow at least twelve weeks.

275. If you are organising a major regional event, allow at least six months.

276. If you are organising a major national event, allow at least twelve months.

277. If you are attending a small, medium, or even regional event, you can probably get away with a pop-up stand and collateral holders.

278. If you are attending a major regional or national event, then try to consider what you could do to make you stand out (no pun intended). This need not cost the earth.

279. If you are doing an event for yourself, always go and check the venue with a checklist – I've included one.

280. Don't believe the venue maps – the whole of Middle England is not conveniently placed for London, Birmingham or Edinburgh.

281. Meet up with your expert speakers beforehand and make sure you know what they're saying.

282. Always do an equipment check beforehand.

283. Always have a back-up plan for key-note speakers, PC's, sound systems, projectors.

284. Carry extra power extension cables.

285. Clearly mark everything that's yours. Things will go 'missing' whilst you're at large events.

286. Make sure wherever possible you have your hand-out leaflets delivered before you get to the event. Parcels tend to go missing because of the sheer size of some events.

287. Be prepared to be flexible when you arrive at an event and find your stand space is the wrong size, in the wrong space, etc. Don't panic… just adapt.

288. Be prepared to tear a strip off the event managers for not doing what they've agreed to. Manufactured anger is a key tool in your tool-box.

289. Storage space at events is at a premium. Make sure all your 'kit' is stored in easily accessible crates and is clearly marked.

290. Don't turn up one minute before the event opens and expect the electricity to be switched on to your stand, even if it was all working last night.

291. If you're making videos at an event, make sure your Terms & Conditions are clearly explained and fully understood by your team.

292. Make sure you've briefed your team on how to handle The Press.

293. Watch out for your competitors who will always appear and try to create PR problems from what you tell them.

294. No-one can survive on coffee for eight hours. Polo Mints do not count as a food group. Make sure everyone takes a break.

295. Make sure your event team take breaks and lunches in shifts.

296. Creating 'stand-out' might seem expensive, but needn't be… it's all about 'razzle dazzle'. When a magician get's up on stage, he or she uses stage props for their show. That's what you've got to do.

297. Another method of creating stand-out is to use lighting. Lights can create depth, shadows, highlighting products, spotlighting speakers, and creating the illusion of shapes against any plain backdrop. How do you think quiz shows or Question Time with Dimbleby works?

298. Don't let the Sales staff slope off. They're almost certain to turn up late and want to be away early. This means you have the delight of setting up on your own and breaking your stand down with no help.

299. Don't let the Salespeople think the event is a 'jolly'. Don't let them stroll in after a night out half-cut and half dead from lack of sleep.

300. Always carry 'Resolve' or another hangover cure, because Salespeople will always 'try it on' no matter what you do.

301. When asking customers to an event, get them to agree in writing – text, faxback form, email, web form… it doesn't matter which. People who agree in writing are 32% more likely to attend. Agreement in writing increases commitment.

302. The most important thing you can take to an event is a comfortable pair of shoes. You'll be on your feet a long time…

303. …and don't sit down. Sitting down signals you're 'not interested' and shows 'I don't respect you enough to stand for you' to potential customers.

304. The second important thing to take is comfy underwear. Trust me… it really is.

305. Don't expect to get everything right… you won't.

306. Event organisers will always have space left. If you can, leave booking your stand until six weeks before the date… but prepare in any case.

307. If you can afford it, and it's a major event, use a stand design company. Get them to set up the stand beforehand.

308. Keep a list of things you need for the event. When you find you've missed something, add it for next time.

309. It's tempting to get plastered on the evenings. Don't. People don't like Beer breath. If you must have a few drinks, make sure you have Mints for the following day.

310. If you have to stay in a hotel… take some earplugs. There's nothing worse than a bad night's sleep before an event.

311. If you need one, don't forget a razor.

312. If it's an 'official' event, don't forget your tie.

313. Things will go wrong… make sure you have an emergency box – duct tape, stapler, pens, paper, USB stick, lead forms, calculator, etc.

314. It will be hot in an event. Take some bottled water.

315. Create a staff briefing document for your event team. Send it to them to read four to five days before going to the event. Take them through it two to three days before.

316. Hold a final stand briefing on the day of the event to remind your staff of what they need to do. Ensure your team knows where the toilets and the refreshments are.

317. Smile at the attendees.

318. Wear the appropriate clothes. T-shirts for general public… suits for public bodies.

319. Have a plan for the event. Know what message you want to get across to your attendees. Know what you want to get out of the day/days. Know what success looks like. Know how you'll measure success.

320. If you have give-aways, make sure they're relevant to the message you want to get across to your attendees.

321. If you have collateral (brochures, leaflets, etc.), make sure you have collateral stands.

322. People who drink caffeine before reading a proposal are 35% more likely to be well disposed toward that proposal (assuming that proposal is rational or course).

323. Ensure you have somewhere for your coats, jackets and laptop bags that can be locked.

324. Plan how attendees will approach and interact with your stand.

325. Link up to the Internet. Show attendees information on your website, if you have no collateral available on the day.

326. Have a printer linked up to your PC and Internet, so you can print out information on product or services, that you don't have any collateral for on the day.

327. Take cash to cover expenses. Always ask for a receipt.

328. If you can afford it, outsource any collateral design and creation. You can do without having to do it on top of the stand organisation and logistics.

329. Use your stand as a large piece of collateral. It's just another stage prop for your show.

330. Always have a stand manager available to deal with emergencies.

331. Get yourself trained in dealing with journalists. You will say something, and you will see it on Twitter twenty minutes later.

332. Use your own Twitter, Facebook and LinkedIn accounts during the show to provide PR to your followers.

333. If you can afford it, provide coffee or sweets for the people approaching your stand.

334. If the event organisers have barcode scanners for scanning the attendee's badges, hire them. They may cost you money, but they save a ton of time writing out leads forms.

335. Have a storage cupboard for collateral.

336. Set up a digital video camera and interview attendees. Use the video on your emails and website. Make sure the background has your logo on it.

337. Book travel tickets in advance to get the best prices.

338. Don't attempt to take major stand items by train.

339. Make sure your overnight bag has wheels… even the lightest shoulder bags get heavy after a while.

340. If the event is in London, cross-town traffic will mean it takes you at least an hour to get to the rail station at peak rush-hour.

341. Don't turn up 30 minutes before the event is due to open and start setting up your stand. The people who do are numpties (Geordie slang for Idiots), and look highly unprofessional.

342. Take some time to have a look around the exhibition yourself. You never know what ideas you'll get for future events from your colleagues.

343. If you have arranged to run a seminar, make sure your speaker has at least four weeks' notice. Give your speaker a deadline of five days before the event to have the seminar presentation/script ready.

344. Checklist for venues

- ☐ Room Height for show stand?
- ☐ Power points for equipment?
- ☐ Number of powerpoints?
- ☐ Power points easily reached?
- ☐ Can they provide tablecloths?
- ☐ Tables?
- ☐ Easy access for clients?
- ☐ Easy access for equipment?
- ☐ Access times okay?
- ☐ Easily found?
- ☐ Map of road system?
- ☐ Days and dates okay?
- ☐ Refreshments?
- ☐ Light food?
- ☐ Buffet?

345. Checklist for event

- ☐ Show stand
- ☐ Show stand panels
- ☐ Offer leaflet
- ☐ Give-aways
- ☐ Product & Service brochures
- ☐ PC's
- ☐ Access to the Internet
- ☐ Linked-up printer
- ☐ Printer paper
- ☐ Ink cartridges
- ☐ Power cables
- ☐ Extension blocks and 4-gangs
- ☐ Barcode pens

- ☐ 'A' Board
- ☐ 'A' Board posters
- ☐ T-shirts (pre-labeled for staff)
- ☐ Travel
- ☐ Accommodation
- ☐ Staff document
- ☐ Directions to hotel
- ☐ Direction to venue
- ☐ Clip board
- ☐ Glue gun
- ☐ Internet connection
- ☐ Computers
- ☐ Computer speakers
- ☐ MS software
- ☐ Product software
- ☐ Small cutting board
- ☐ Extension leads
- ☐ USB stick
- ☐ Projector
- ☐ Projector bulbs
- ☐ Pull up literature racks
- ☐ Pull up stands
- ☐ Lectern
- ☐ Room direction signs
- ☐ Inside room signs
- ☐ Banner signs for outside?
- ☐ Foam core
- ☐ Spray mount
- ☐ Cellotape
- ☐ Power cables
- ☐ Small notepad
- ☐ Laptop
- ☐ Blue tack
- ☐ Pens
- ☐ Pencils
- ☐ Pads
- ☐ Highlighter
- ☐ Stapler
- ☐ Staples
- ☐ Ruler
- ☐ Knife
- ☐ Scissors

- ☐ Badges
- ☐ Badge holders
- ☐ Blank badges
- ☐ Arrange refreshments
- ☐ Arrange food
- ☐ Arrange information packs
- ☐ Arrange 'gifts'
- ☐ Arrange 'on the day' offers

346. Event Mailer

- ☐ Write mailer
- ☐ Third party logo's
- ☐ Design Response form
- ☐ Arrange labels
- ☐ Arrange envelope filling
- ☐ Arrange postage
- ☐ Arrange tele-appointing follow-up
- ☐ Create list of attendee's

347. Event Presentation

- ☐ Equipment test
- ☐ Spare equipment
- ☐ Who will present?
- ☐ Fits the schedule?

348. Third Parties

- ☐ Know where they're going?
- ☐ Know when they're presenting?
- ☐ Know your schedule?
- ☐ Speakers arranged

349. On the day

- ☐ Guides to shepherd attendees in the right direction
- ☐ Receptionist
- ☐ Sales people on day
- ☐ Contact list for all staff

350. Personal Checklist

- ☐ Comfy black shoes
- ☐ Socks
- ☐ Two pairs of black trousers
- ☐ Deodorant
- ☐ Breath freshener/mints
- ☐ Razors
- ☐ Shaving foam
- ☐ Old t-shirt (to wear for stand assembly)
- ☐ Ear-plugs (for hotel nights)
- ☐ At least one change of casual clothes per day
- ☐ Tube Map
- ☐ £70 in cash
- ☐ Credit/Debit card
- ☐ Mobile (with credit)
- ☐ Book
- ☐ MP3 Player
- ☐ Sleeping tablets
- ☐ Small scissors
- ☐ Needle and thread
- ☐ Travel toothbrush
- ☐ Toothpaste
- ☐ Brush/Comb
- ☐ Mobile charger
- ☐ Tube map
- ☐ Taxi numbers
- ☐ Contacts for support personnel

351. Always make sure you know what your objectives are, and how you'll measure them.

352. Provide your team with as much background audience, product and event knowledge as possible before the event.

353. Lists... lists... lists. Use them and you can't go wrong.

354. Events are 75% logistics. The actual event day itself is just the culmination of a lot of hard work.

355. Give your team two briefings. The first one a week before the event. The second one on the day of the event, thirty minutes before you are due to open.

356. Arrange your travel as far in advance as possible to get the best prices.

357. Accommodation – make sure you check out your accommodation before you get there. Don't be put up in the hotel with paper-thin walls and the potential for prostitution or the mad axe-man sleeping (or not) next door to you.

Websites

These days, websites are essential to any marketing effort. Why? Quite simply you can track and make changes almost instantaneously, and I hope by now you've realised I believe marketing is about understanding results and evolving what you're doing.

358. Know what you want to get out of your website. Is it sales? Stats? Leads? Views?

359. A 'bounce' is where a visitor lands on your website and 'bounces' off within the first ten seconds.

360. Keep it simple. The more complex you make it, the more likely the visitor will bounce.

361. A good rule of thumb is that anything less than a 50% bounce rate is working reasonable well. You can then evolve your designs to continually reduce this level.

362. A website is not a magazine. Don't put an editorial on the landing page. Put directions to what the visitor wants there.

363. Make sure whatever the visitor wants is only one or two clicks away from where they land. Seeing an immediate link to what the visitor wants reduces bounce. A good example of this are the immediate links on Amazon.

364. Personalised landing pages reduce bounce. It's a fact that the more a reader sees their name in the text, the more likely they are to read on.

365. Make sure you have Google analytics aligned to your site. It's free, and you'll get masses of market intelligence within a very short time. It will also guide you on what to evolve to reduce bounce rates per page.

366. What can you add to a website? Product tours; Whitepaper download; How to Guides; Software trials; Discussion Forum's; Videos; Podcasts; News; Competitions; Surveys; Adverts for your products/services.

Email

Despite the introduction of all sorts of social media, email remains – and will continue to remain in my opinion – the staple tool of marketing for many years to come.

367. First, foremost, always, get the customer or prospects permission to email them.

368. Secondly, make sure that even if you do have the customer or prospects permission to email them, that what you are sending them what they gave you the permission to do.

369. If you get their permission to email them, and what you're sending them is what they've asked for, then what you're sending them is not spam.

370. By UK law, you are currently allowed to send them emails to try to get them to give you their permission… but you are not allowed to actively sell to them.

371. Why get their permission? Why only send them what they've asked for? Because email is about building a lifetime/lifecycle relationship with your customer or prospect, so that you get to talk to them about what you want, and they get to hear about things that they might be interested in.

372. If you send them emails that aren't relevant to their needs, or you sell their details to the highest bidder, you are going to have seriously unhappy contacts, and the least you'll get away with is being put on a spam register. What's the maximum that could happen to you? Well, let's just say that you could be awaiting Her Majesty's pleasure.

373. Always check whether your contact is TPS (Telephone Preference Service) MPS (the Mailing Preference Service) or the FPS (Fax Preference

Services). If they are, then you can't contact them by telephone or mail to get their email permission.

374. When sending emails to customers or prospects, always give them the option to unsubscribe. This might, on first hearing it, sound like lunacy… why on earth would you do this? But consider, every time you use a bulk emailer (and I'm assuming you'll be using one to send out tens, if not hundreds or thousands of emails) you will be charged for that email, and all you'll do is wind drive that contact round the bend. You'll never sell to them, and you're wasting your own money too.

375. The subject line is the line that appears on your email system before you've opened the email.

376. The body is the email itself, the bit that you open to read.

377. The footer is the last part of the email. The bit that usually has all the Terms & Conditions, the unsubscribe, and any mandatory links.

378. Always make your subject line relevant to the body copy. If you don't do this, your email could be interpreted as spam.

379. Email results are easy to track, so the more you do, and the more you understand what causes a response in your customers and prospects, the better your emails will become when you evolve them.

380. To see instant results, you can buy credits with an off-the-peg web-email supplier. These companies provide you with the ability to bulk-email and usually provide you with all the stats you could wish for. You'll be able to see when your email landed, who opened your email, where they clicked through to, etc., and if you've linked this up to website analytics, you'll be able to continue their journey right through to download or sale. And the more you see this, the easier it is to understand your customer or prospect.

381. Effective email is targeted email. So the more you know about your customer or prospect, the more you can target your message to their precise needs.

382. People who buy products advertised in emails spend 138% more than those who don't buy through emails.

383. Test, test, test. Wherever possible, test headlines, pricing, industry groups, offers, click through's. Every test helps you get better the next time around.

384. Keep a track of your testing. This is your bank of knowledge for increasing your results and increasing your bonus/profit/pay.

385. Cut costs. If you can prove through testing that your customers or prospects don't need hard copy marketing anymore, move your messaging to email.

386. But the key word in is 'prove'.

387. Customers still need a catalogue to look at? Send them, via email, to a 'turn-page technology' catalogue that they can 'flip' through on screen.

388. Even better, embed links to downloads, more information, and your online store directly into your email or turn-page technology brochure.

389. Email ROI (Return on Investment – not to be confused with The Republic of Ireland) is 70% higher than any other Direct Marketing medium.

390. Email delivers sales at roughly 10% of the cost of a website banner advert.

391. Email delivers sales at roughly 25% of the cost of paid for search.

392. Email delivers sales at 30% of the cost of affiliate advertising.

393. But… email is at its most effective when used alongside other marketing tools such as Direct Mail.

394. Know the rules of email content. This is actually what the customer or prospect is thinking when they read your email:

- What do I have to do?
- Can you show me what you're talking about?
- How often are we going to be talking?
- What's in this relationship for me?
- How well do you want to get to know me?
- Should I trust you?
- Is this easy for me to do?
- Can you confirm that I've done what I think you wanted?

395. Close observers will see that this isn't so much different from the AIDCA principles of copywriting. The main difference is its immediacy, and the fact that there doesn't have to be a salesperson physically involved.

396. Or does there? Companies are now starting to use web-chat.

What's web-chat?

Web-chat is the ability to see, in real time, where someone is on your website. Not only that… you can ask them, again in real time via a two-way text box, if they would like any help, and guide them toward the right solution for them, just like a shop assistant. Scary! And a technical support/customer service person can handle up to four visitors at any one time.

397. Keep your email lists clean – Make it your mission to regularly remove bounces, unsubscribed, and generic addresses such as 'sales@'. By leaving them in, all you're doing is wasting your own money if you're using a bulk emailer, and skewing your ROI.

398. By keeping your lists clean, there's also less likelihood that you'll be seen as a spammer by your ISP, and that a disgruntled reader will report you as one.

399. Always give your audience the option to 'forward the email to a friend'.

400. Always include links to your privacy policy.

401. If they unsubscribe, set up a re-subscribe 'sorry you're leaving us' cycle with an stay-with-us offer.

402. Segment your email lists to create more relevant copy and increase ROI.

403. But don't just segment them along Industry code lines. Why not segment them on how much activity you've seen from them. For example, are they close to buying? Have you seen them, over time, download a brochure, take a test drive of your product, and scan the offer pages on your website? What makes this segment buy would be radically different from someone who has simply downloaded a free Top Tips sheet.

404. If you're trying to get leads via email, use short copy.

405. If you're trying to sell immediately… still use short copy, but get them to click through to more extensive copy on your website.

406. Normal rules apply… you have two seconds to interest a prospect, and five seconds for a customer.

407. 'Above-the-fold' is an archaic term from the news-trade industry that is still in use. It used to mean any headline that was on the front page of the newspaper, above where it was folded in half, when it was handed to you by the newspaper seller on the street.

408. Today it's more current use refers to anything that can be seen within your email window without having to scroll down.

409. Make sure the most important elements of what you need to say to gain the audience interest are above-the-fold in your email.

410. Without doubt, the most important aspect of any email campaign is the subject line. If you haven't interested your audience in the subject line, they'll never even open your email.

411. Make your email layout as easy and clear as possible for your audience to act upon.

412. Use email newsletters to build long term relationships. Don't make the mistake of burning your relationship all in one go by 'sell, sell, sell' tactics.

413. Provide regular news items of added-value to your audience through newsletters.

414. Sit 'soft sell' messages alongside these added-value news items.

415. Newsletters are ideal for cross-selling, and up-selling.

416. Newsletters are ideal for creating exclusivity.

417. Tease your newsletter audience by only showing part of a story. Have the remainder available on your website if the audience clicks through.

418. Establish frequency of emails. Track responses over time for patterns. Segment accordingly, and target your copy more efficiently.

419. Unless you have breaking news, don't send emails more frequently than every 48 hours.

420. If you're going to personalise your emails, for God's sake test them first. There's nothing more credibility sapping than seeing 'Dear <first name>' on an email.

421. Subject lines – short and snappy seems to work the best. Research shows subject lines with less than 50 characters are the norm, but this seems to be shortening as time goes by.

422. To become an adept at short subject lines, you can find no better training that looking at Japanese Haiku poems. They cram so much into such a short space, yet paint you a picture that you see instantly.

For example – "old pond . . . a frog leaps in, water's sound".

423. Your business brand is immensely important. The stronger your brand, the more trustworthy you are seen to be, and the more likely the audience is to open your email.

424. Avoid ambiguous headlines like 'monthly newsletter'. They mean nothing to most readers and have very low opening rates.

425. Strong offers encourage open rates. Especially subject lines with 'free' and 'new'. However, always use a spam checker to make sure your email doesn't get filtered out by using these words.

426. In promotional emails, the audience is expecting an offer, so don't be shy. If there's an end date, don't hesitate to use it, even in the subject line. For example 'Great shoe sale – must end 30th June'

427. Be honest – The temptation is always there to get your reader to open the email by whatever means, and then deal with them. Don't. You're only storing up irritation and resentment in the customer. They'll never buy from you in any case, because you've blown your credibility.

428. Don't forget the 'From' line. Customers are naturally skeptic of 'From' email addresses that don't seem to come from the company they say they're from. Of course, you're not emailing with criminal intent, it

usually means that you're using a bulk emailer, so make sure your company name/your name is in this line, rather than your provider.

429. Always, always, ask the reader to do something. Readers who read, but don't do anything will not give you any metrics to evolve your campaigns.

430. Trial text only versus graphic emails. In many cases graphic emails are seen as 'selling emails' whereas text emails are seen as 'personal messages'. This varies from audience to audience and also pulls in brand reputation and frequency of contact, so the only way to be certain is to… yes, you guessed it, test.

431. If a customer goes onto your web shop, registers, but doesn't buy, why not have automated emails ready, that go out to them a day or so later. You could ask if they found all the information they needed, or you could even simply make them an offer.

432. Avoid 'do not reply' type messages. These can be a real turn off to a customer expecting exceptional customer service.

433. Images in emails don't always show up. Always test your emails in Google mail, Yahoo, AOL, and whatever other email provider is the latest fashion.

434. Always ask your reader to place you on their trusted email list. That way, your emails will always get through.

435. Make sure your emails are all printer-friendly… people still like to see their emails printed out.

436. What will your email look like in a mobile phone? You don't know? Well, you better find out because that's the way it's going/gone!

437. Regularly review your campaigns and cycles. There's nothing worse than seeing the same creative. When this happens, you know you've embedded a schema in

the mind of the customer that you need to break again.

438. In direct mail a second offer to the same audience within 30 days of the first will pull 40-50% of the initial response. This remains broadly true for email campaigns as well.

439. Stop, stop! You'll burn out the lists! What rubbish. The only way you burn out a list is by sending them something that isn't relevant to them. As long as you're abiding by what you say you will in your privacy agreement, and as long as the audience finds what you're sending them useful, they'll accept your emails.

440. The perfect example of this is 'Word a Day' that sends out, quite literally, the meaning of a word each day to over 200,000 contacts. Are they sick to death of receiving an email today? Well, some might be, but I'd bet the vast majority find the information relevant to themselves and are quite happy to receive it.

441. You only remember that you've sent your audience six emails in the last three months because you are in control. People forget what happened last week, never mind two months ago. They're more interested in how they'll get the revenue in this week, or how they'll spend their summer holidays, or how to stop their kid from getting into the wrong crowd.

442. But… permission does fade over time, so you need to make sure your audience has the option to opt-out. So how do you know you've stopped being relevant to your customers? You monitor the opt-outs.

443. Even better than monitoring your opt-out. Ask your audience how often they'd like to hear from you. That way you're dancing to their tune, and it's a tune they're happy to hear.

Data

Data is the single most important element of a campaign you need to get right. Good data will save poor copywriting. Good data will reduce the need for an offer. Poor data will ensure your campaign needs all the luck and skill it can get to make it work.

444. Establish who you've already sold to, then make a profile of your best customers. Use this profile to find 'look-a-likes' in your existing customer base and new prospect data lists.

445. Rank your 'look-a-like' data into priority order, and start using the data from the highest priority downwards.

446. You are better off sending two-thousand mailers to a highly targeted list, than twenty-thousand to a poorly targeted list… the results will be about the same, and you'll have saved yourself eighteen-thousand second class postage costs and printing, or email payments.

447. Don't over mail all in one go. Find out how much response your salespeople can accept at any one time.

448. Only send out more/less than this amount if:

    a) your rate of mailing theory has been proved wrong, i.e.: your salespeople are finding they can handle more/less, or their conversion rate is increasing/decreasing, or your open up rate (or estimate) has increased/decreased

    b) you are under political pressure to 'be seen to be mailing more'.

449. From your previous campaigns find out what conversion to lead you are creating.

450. From your previous campaigns find out (or estimate) what your open up rate is.

451. From the amount of response your salespeople can accept, work backwards, through conversion and open up rate, to find out how much data you need to send out at any one time.

452. If you need to 'be seen to be mailing more', then there is something wrong with someone's management systems.

453. The reason being 'seen to mail more' is wrong, is because your percentage open up rate will drop, the further away from the norm your look-a-like data is. It follows that you'll get worse results… but crucially, your spending the same amount of money to get those results. All this does is bring down you Return on Investment (ROI), and your Cost per Order (CPO).

454. In general, the more focused and targeted you can make your copywriting and offer, the better your sales will be. So it's in your own best interests to define your data as much as possible, to help you establish what offers and copy would be most relevant to that data.

455. Remember though… the more you segment, the more you will have to individualise your copy and offer. If you move from one batch of data, to ten batches of segmented data, you'll have to create ten different messages.

456. Rubbish in, rubbish out. If your data is flaky, your impact will be too.

457. The only thing worse than no information is bad information. No information 'might' cost you responses… bad information 'will' cost you money.

458. Check frequency of purchase to establish when to contact customers.

459. Analyze your data and establish a frequent buyer programme to maintain loyalty.

460. Establish the 'lifetime value' of a customer by analyzing your data. That way you will always be aware of how much you could potentially lose if you don't take care of them.

461. There are two kinds of database customers

a) transactional – where it's simply a one-off sale

b) relationship – where you want an ongoing relationship with your customer in order to make more than one sale

462. You need to know which is which in order to build loyalty with one, and incentivise the other.

463. Never believe a database modeling result without a) evaluating it with focus groups and b) testing your assumptions with real life trials.

464. Don't talk technical to a tekky, you'll look daft. Always ask for their 'valuable advice' and always remember to say that you're probably 'asking a daft question'.

465. Don't assume that all your worries will be solved if you can only get an analyst to analyse your data. You will probably find that you have more information but 'know' less.

466. Getting trained on data-analysis software is great, as long as you keep using the software. Otherwise, it's just a waste of your time because you won't use it frequently enough for it to become second nature.

467. Always give an analyst your objectives. Never let them come up with 'interesting facts' for the sake of it.

468. Improve your ROI immediately – only market to your top 30% of data based on propensity to buy.

Testing…

What can you learn from Darwin?

469. Marketing is not about fluffy pictures. If you want fluffy pictures, pick up a book on design.

470. Marketing is rarely about radical ideas. If you want radical ideas you need to read a book on philosophy.

471. Marketing is 90% evolution and 10% revolution.

472. When Darwin was asked how evolution could be responsible for the human eye, he replied that it was quite possible, over millions of years, to move from a simple binary eye that saw either black or white, through a series of hundreds of thousands of adaptations that gradually gave multi-point light and dark which created a basic picture, to full three dimensional sight.

     The key factor being time to experiment; time cut out all the genetic failures; time to improve upon the genetic traits that improved the eye-sight.

     You must do exactly the same with your marketing.

     Don't get me wrong. Some evolutions will be great leaps forward, helping boost your response rates by whole percentage points, but the vast majority will be minute changes 'that collectively' will add up to more than the sum of the parts.

Telemarketing and Telesales

A bunch of rogues... but their your rogues

In this chapter I might possibly be seen as being derisory of salespeople. That is very far from my intention.

I try never to forget that salespeople are the final link in the commercial chain.

473. As a marketing person you would like to believe that it's your marketing that's making a difference. You would be wrong. It is a combination of commercial knowledge, data extraction, marketing, and skill at selling, that together, helps persuade the customer to buy.

So marketing people must face reality, unless your product or service sells itself, or unless it is completely web based, you are reliant on a salesperson.

The salesperson helps puts money in your bank at the end of the month. If you want that new car, or the holiday in the sun, you must work with your salespeople.

474. Salespeople are salespeople for one reason, and one reason only… to make money.

475. Nobody comes out of school or college or University saying 'I want to be a salesperson'. Sales is something you fall into because you find you're good at it. For those that do find they're good at it, it's a career that can bring them huge financial rewards.

476. Sales people, who cannot sell, will not be salespeople for long. They'll move on, or they will be moved on.

477. The way to a sales person's heart is through their bonus. Make sure you're giving them their bonus for doing what you want.

478. What you want might not necessarily be just getting sales in.

479. If, halfway through a month, a salesperson knows they will not stand a chance of hitting their bonus, they'll reduce the amount of selling they're doing that month, and start squirreling away potential sales for next month.

480. To avoid salespeople giving up on the month halfway through it, provide them with a daily incentive not to, as well as the monthly bonus. This way, even if the salesperson knows they won't hit their monthly target, they have a very good chance of getting their daily incentive.

481. The daily incentive need not be money, as long as it has a monetary value.

482. The daily incentive need not be guaranteed. It could be entry into a draw. The more times you hit your daily target, the more chance you have of winning at the end of the month.

483. To get the best from salespeople, you have to respect them.

484. To get the best from your salespeople, they must trust you.

485. Trust springs from you understanding them, and from them understanding you.

486. This means that you need to sit with them... listen to them. Join their sales meetings. Keep them up-to-date with your marketing. Be concerned when they have a bad day. More, when they have a bad day, do something about it.

487. Don't forget though… some sales people will always try to find the loop holes that will give them the maximum return, for the minimum effort. You can't blame them… you'd do it too.

488. Find out when the calls come in. Look for call patterns. Are more calls coming in on a Wednesday than a Monday? Is Friday a really low day? Do calls build up after lunch? When do you make most sales, at the start of the month or the end? Do you make sales immediately after a campaign has landed, or a week later?

489. Get the salespeople used to seeing you. Make sure you go to see how they're doing at least twice per day.

490. Give the salespeople samples from active marketing campaigns, so they know what the customer is talking about.

491. Ensure all marketing material has a source code, so the salesperson can identify it and record it when they take a call.

492. Incentive the salesperson to ask for the marketing codes when a customer calls.

493. Penalise the salesperson for not asking for the marketing codes when a customer calls.

494. Incentives don't have to cost the world. Doughnuts might do!

495. The weekend acts as a natural break in thought for the customer, so try to get mailers landing on a Monday or a Tuesday. This way, it gives the customer five whole days to call inbound. If your mailer lands on a Wednesday at lunchtime, the customer only has two and half days to react.

496. Wednesdays and Thursdays seem to be the best days for emails to land.

497. Emails seem to provoke fairly rapid response – twenty-four hours. Always make sure your salespeople we're provided with the email before it went out.

498. Fridays tend to be slow days in Business-to-Business (B2B). Friday afternoons are the worst part of that day for inbound calls.

499. The weather plays a crucial role in inbound call rates.

During June 2008, the UK had a mini heat wave. The inbound line of the sales team I was working with at the time reduced in direct proportion to the increase in temperature.

I raised this point to colleagues, and was laughed at for my troubles. I was right… six months later I heard a senior executive suggesting the same thing.

What this proves is that if you're ahead of the game, and have factual proof, it doesn't mean to say you'll be believed.

Belief comes from hindsight in career executives.

500. Bank holidays affect inbound sales lines. You will suffer reductions in calls beforehand. You need to factor these into your forecasts.

501. People take extra time off around bank holidays. You will suffer extra reductions in calls in a short week. You need to factor these into your forecasts.

502. The summer holidays affects inbound sales lines. You will suffer reductions in calls beforehand. You need to factor these into your forecasts.

503. The final two weeks before Christmas are dead weeks. You will suffer reductions in calls beforehand. You need to factor these into your forecasts.

504. Schools will not buy from you during the summer holidays. Don't bother mailing them, you're just wasting money.

505. Public authorities spend the last of their budgets in the run up to Financial Year End (the end of March).

506. Public authorities contract to start spending their new budgets following Financial Year End (the end of March).

507. Private companies are more likely to buy two weeks either side of their Financial Year End. These 'new years' are usually January, April, July or October, with January, and April being the preferred times.

Agencies

When I was young and naive, and thought that I knew everything, I used to believe that agencies were out to take your budget, and that all they were interested in was getting you to part with your money.

This isn't always the case.

508. The best agencies can act as an outsourced element of your marketing team. Good account managers can help you immensely, and they can provide you with an insight on how to approach your audience. The saying that 'no man is an island' is nowhere more important than when working alongside an agency.

509. There are two ways to work with agencies:

   a) Tell them what you want
   b) Ask them for ideas

   Both ways are valid, and both ways have positives and negatives attached to them.

510. By telling the agency what exactly you want you are guaranteed to get exactly what you've asked for. This is great… as long as you're certain what you've asked for will work.

511. By asking an agency for ideas, you are asking them to use their experience to provide you with options. This is great… as long as you're certain they have the experience to provide you with the best options.

512. So where does this leave you?

You have to decide whether:

a) You have enough experience to be directive with an agency and ask them for exactly what you want

b) The agency you are considering using has enough experience to be able to give you some good answers to your brief.

513. Quite often there is no right or wrong answer.

But consider. If you are paying an agency substantial fees and having to be directive, isn't that a bit like 'having a Dog and barking yourself'?

So if you are being directive, you need to make sure you're not paying over the odds for creative ideas.

514. Written briefs are a matter of personal taste. Some marketing people find they're good for crystallising your thoughts. Others view them as unnecessary if you give a verbal brief and ask for your agency to provide you with written version in response.

515. Always give a verbal brief. Get your agency to take notes and then come back to you with their version of what you've asked for. This is a safety net to ensure your agency understands what you said.

516. Always give your agency the 'mandatory items' you need to see – branding, logo, telephone numbers, web addresses, etc.

517. Always give your agency the success criteria for your campaign. That way they'll know what you're trying to achieve overall.

518. Always give your agency a view of the audience your campaign is going out to. That way their creative

team will be able to create a mood board. This will help them get in tune with who they're talking to.

519. Always agree the costs in advance, stating clearly what you expect to pay and when you expect to do so.

520. Always agree timelines in advance, stating clearly when you expect to see creative.

521. Local agencies tend to be flexible with making alterations to your creative, in many cases even after they thought you'd agreed a final version. Sometimes they won't even charge you for this. National agencies will not do this! National agencies charge by the hour and will usually agree two batches of alterations (or alts) in with the costs, and every time you make more alts, they'll carry on charging by the hour.

522. Always be polite to your account manager. They can pull your arse out of the fire if you are in trouble and need some creative produced in a hurry.

523. Never be afraid to say you don't like agency creative… but always be prepared for your account manager to ask what it is you don't like about it.

524. In pitch situations, agencies will always have a preferred creative option. Be aware of this. They might put less effort into the secondary options and try to persuade you to go for their preference because they've put so much effort into it. Effort is not the right reason to go for something. Whether it fulfils your brief is the reason you should go with a creative option.

525. What is the aim of a good account manager? The best account managers want to:

   a. Give you what you want

   b. Do it for as little cost as they can get away with.

Why is this important? It's important because the best account managers will question, and question, and question you, drawing every last detail of what you're after out of you, because their aim is to get maximum reward for minimum outlay. In their business, time is money.

So if an account manager isn't putting you on the rack when taking a brief, they're not doing their job properly.

Ideas

Some people believe that you have to be naturally gifted to have ideas. I want to tell you here and now that that's rubbish.

Back in the 1960's a gentleman named James Webb Young was asked to establish how a team of businessmen (because it was business-men back then) could generate ideas.

526. James Webb Young established that generating ideas was actually quite simple:

a) Collate as much information as possible on your subject.

b) Read through your information. Let your conscious mind understand and absorb the subject.

c) Then do something unexpected… set your information aside and deliberately do not think about it. This allows your unconscious mind to mull over the possibilities.

d) Return to the subject after time has elapsed. You will find that it is easier to 'see' connections. This is because your brain… your mind… is an astoundingly good possibility engine. It can silently compute thousands of options and possibilities 'in the background' whilst you are carrying on your normal working day, or indeed, having a good night's sleep.

That's all!

527. The fact is that the majority of ideas are old ideas that have been combined together to form something new.

528. No idea is bad. The only bad ideas are the ones that never make it off the drawing board.

529. The best ideas are often the most simple. These ideas are usually evolutionary ideas.

530. Evolutionary ideas will be accepted more easily by your present audiences.

531. The problem with evolutionary ideas is that everyone else, given the same facts, will have the same idea. They're sensible, and logical, and reasonable.

532. Reasonable works well, but you only get reasonable results.

533. To have revolutionary ideas you have to take unsafe decisions. Only by taking these decisions will you break the logic of the evolutionary route.

534. In 'Terminator' starring Arnie, the rise of thinking robots is started by a programmer who builds into their program the coding 'Take a chance'. This offers the opportunity for them to make a illogical decision.

You need to do the same every now and again. Who knows, it might work! And it might work better than anything you've ever done before.

535. Revolutionary ideas will almost always be criticised by the 'old guard'. If you have the strength of your convictions, ignore your critics.

536. Revolutionary ideas are quite often the complete polar opposite of existing ideas, for example: The Fosbury Flop; The Dyson Vacuum Cleaner; The Blair-Witch Project;

537. Revolutionary ideas can be quirky, insane, heretical, random… until they're accepted, after which they become the old ideas.

538. In 'Journeyer', the novel by Gary Jennings, Marco Polo tells the reader that the saddest thing he had ever heard was hearing his cell mate say "I always wished I had done this, or that… but I never did."

It's better to regret doing something, than to wish you had done it, but find out it's too late.

539. But… you still need Intent, and you still need objectives, and you still need success criteria. If you become a revolutionary without these, you're not harnessing your idea powers to a goal… you're just being a spoiled brat or an anarchist.

Where the hell's the middle man gone?

Gone are the days when you could produce a product, or provide a service, and force it on your customer because your customer has no choice but to accept it.

Back in the old days – less than twenty years ago – it was still possible to do this. After all, you, as the seller, controlled the four P's.

You controlled the Product – it was your design and that's what you'd made available.

You controlled the Place – you made it available through channels to market that you had selected.

You controlled the Price – you sold it at the price that you wanted, and you made the profit that you'd forecast.

And you controlled the Promotion – you controlled the advertising and marketing that your buyer saw.

In short, your potential buyer had no choice.

If the buyer wanted a product or a service, they had very few to choose from. It would be rare that a buyer had enough capital to create exactly what they wanted.

If the buyer wanted a product or a service, they had to go to the sellers chosen channel to buy it. There were very few alternatives.

If the buyer wanted a product or a service, they had to pay the price you had set. Otherwise they couldn't buy.

If the buyer wanted a product or a service, they learnt about it through a limited number of promotions. Only sellers with capital could afford these promotions.

And, crucially, what would happen if your buyer wished to complain? Well… who cared? It would be rare that the buyer would have access to a channel of complaint that could seriously affect your future sales. And if they did – perhaps a Watchdog TV programme – then the buyer could be handled by exception rather than the rule.

Plus… even if you weren't happy with your purchase, if you had to use it, you had to use it. What choice did you have? Your buyer suffered in silence because he or she knew they had no choice.
All this has changed drastically.

540. Today, if you are a seller, you need to dance to your customer's tune. The balance of power has swung completely in favour of the buyer. Get used to it.

541. Today the customer sits within a defensive ring that helps them filter out all the spam, and the selling messages that they don't want to hear. That defensive ring is called the Internet.

Let's think about that for a few seconds.

Even ten years ago, if you wanted to check out a hotel that you were considering, where did you go? You went to the travel agents in town. These days what do you do? You open up your laptop – or increasingly, switch on your mobile phone – and check the hotel out on Trip Advisor. Which is easier? Which stops you being pro-actively sold to? The Internet has filtered out all the seller's attempts to force you to listen. You, as the buyer, only listen to the messages you want to hear.

You want house insurance? Years ago you might have called a local broker. These days you hop on

Money Supermarket for (relatively) instant comparisons of hundreds of providers, or you seek advice on best buys from MoneySavingExpert customers who have direct experience – both good and bad – of the service providers.

542. Today, your buyer has access to a huge array of online filter devices that can help them choose between sellers. Here is just a small selection of them:

- Twitter
- YouTube
- Industry websites
- Advisory bodies
- Governmental help
- Customer review websites
- Blogs
- Comparison websites
- Podcasts
- On-demand guides
- Downloadable business whitepapers
- Web chat

You can do absolutely nothing about this! You can't shut them down. You can't muzzle them. You can't afford to buy them out.

You can no longer force your product or service on the customer – they've got the whole world to choose from online.

You can no longer command the price – your customer will get something similar or better from a rival, perhaps in India, perhaps down the road from someone in the home office that you've never even heard of.

You cannot control where people see your advert – gone are the days when you could be certain your customer was watching the commercial break between two halves of Coronation Street. These days your customer might be watching one of five-hundred channels on Cable or Sky, or they could be watching BBC iPlayer, or ITVPlayer, or watching YouTube, or paying on-demand for a movie, or writing their own personal blog, talking in real time to their son in Australia on video Skype, or… well, you get the picture.

You can't even be certain that your promotion will be effective – your customer might compare your offer with fifty or sixty others and find yours comes a poor forty-fifth.

543. And boy oh boy… if your customers want to complain. Well, let's just say, they have access to quite literally thousands of forums in which they can.

There used to be a saying – Do a good job, and the customer will tell one other person; do a bad job and they'll tell twenty.

This saying is outdated. These days they can tell thousands, fairly instantly. And those thousands can each tell thousands more… and suddenly your reputation is in tatters.

And the above should also explain to you why our bricks-and-mortar retail society – the culture of going into town to buy something – is dying.

Not for nothing is the title of this chapter 'Where the hell's the middleman gone?'

The middleman has disappeared because your customers are no longer willing to pay someone a percentage to provide them with something they can get for themselves, simply, quickly, on recommendation, from the Internet.

You need to take a trip 'back to the future'.

Stay with me – it will make sense.

Long before the advent of the Internet, before Logie Baird invented the television, before Thomas Newcomen invented the Steam Engine, Babbage invented the Computer, and before the mass production of newspapers, sellers and buyers actually to talk to each other.

Hard to believe isn't it.

Traders used to meet buyers in the local market place; business men used to discuss the latest prices in pubs and coffee houses; people used to make one-off transactions with sellers; house-wives used to make requests of travelling salesmen for items that they would buy on the salesman's next visit.

It was a two-way conversation.

It was a one-to-one, peer-to-peer, equal-to-equal transaction.

It was a unique, one-off purchase that was tailored to the buyer.

The seller listened to what the buyer wanted, and then supplied it.

The buyer was happy because he or she had got what they had asked for. If they were not happy, they knew who to complain to, and if they were still not happy, they would vote with their feet and not buy from the seller again.

All this changed with the Industrial Revolution.

During the Industrial Revolution, rather than continue with one-to-one, peer-to-peer trading, sellers with capital started to invest in one-to-many forms of communication and mass production.

These new one-to-many production and communication channels usually took large amounts of capital, so the people who could afford to do so were usually the people who already had money, and they reaped the economy of scale benefits that followed.

They changed an equal-to-equal transaction into an enforced sale.

That's why, of the top hundred richest people of the last two-thousand years, twenty-eight of them come from the 1830's and the 1840's, precisely the time when the industrial Revolution was taking place.

And, because these sellers had invested so heavily in bringing down the production costs, and reaching as wide an audience as possible, they were able to squeeze the traditional craftsmen out of business.

Basically, if you didn't have a USP (unique selling point) as a craftsman, you were in trouble.

Many traditional sellers converted to become middlemen, and many others saw an opportunity to buy in bulk from a manufacturer and sell the products down the line at a percentage profit.

This era saw the rise of people like Marks and Spencer, and Fortnum and Mason, and Woolworth, and Binns, and your local department stores around the country.

The common buyer could have anything they wanted, as long as it was what the producer provided, and the middleman was prepared to sell for a percentage.

"You can have it in any colour as long as it's black."

And where did you find out about these products and services? From the mass produced newspapers of course, or, later on, from the radio, or on one of the two or three TV channels that were all you could tune in to.

But now… now, for the first time in around one-hundred and fifty years, the pendulum has swung back to how it was.

Today, the set up costs for an online company are negligible. Anyone can do it. Technology has created a level playing field that the super-rich seller can't compete with. And that's why you have so many rivals who are chipping away at your market share and your profits.

Today, your customer can get a review or complain anytime they like, so you have to take each and every customer seriously.

You have gone back to the future. You have to actually talk, and negotiate for each customer's money. Otherwise you're going the way of the Dinosaur.

So, the lesson for me is clear, if you want to survive as a seller in today's world, you need to stop 'telling' and start 'listening' and 'influencing'.

As a seller you need to start embedding yourself 'with the enemy'.

Did I say 'enemy'? I meant 'my good customer who pays my bills, and puts bread on my table, and clothes on the back of my kids at the end of each month – how can I help you dear sir or madam?'

Buyers of the World Unite. You have nothing to lose but your hard earned cash, so screw the seller into the ground.

Sounds depressing for the seller doesn't it?

It is… but only if you keep up with your present attitude.

So what can you do?

544. You need to ask your customer's permission to talk to them. By asking permission you're treating them with respect. Your customers deserve respect… they're the ones with the cash.

545. You need to engage with your customers in a two way conversation. By engaging with them – and that means no overt 'selling' – you'll show them that you are knowledgeable about their situation and their issues, plus you gain genuine insight into their needs, and their values.

546. You need to start taking part in the web chats that influence your customers. This costs you nothing except time, and it puts you in their space.

547. You need to start providing free demonstrations of your product or service to help provide confidence in it. You need to offer free advice and information without any hooks.

548. You need to start putting up video on YouTube. Video is everywhere these days. The price of making video has dropped from thousand's, to under fifty pounds. Take advantage. It doesn't matter if you're not an expert with a video recorder. Today's audience wants real-life, not tasteful.

549. You need to provide case-studies and testimonials from your existing satisfied customers on the Internet. Potential customers always say that they take no notice of customer testimonials, but research says otherwise.

550. Because the 'Long Tail' means that there will always be someone, somewhere in the world who wants your products, you need to decide whether you want to specialize, or stack it high sell it cheap.

551. The World Wide Web is always on... so you need to make sure that day or night, you have processes in place to respond to customers.

552. Once you have a website store that you know works, the quickest way to increase your sales is to use Google Adwords.

No bragging please we're British…

…or how to get the credit you deserve

In "King Rat" by James Clavell, a book about prisoners in Singapore during World War II, the main character, an Englishman is being cooked breakfast by his American friend.

The American offers him Poached eggs… a luxury that no-one else in the camp can afford… and as Peter is tucking into them, his mouth watering, the American asks 'how are they?'

Peter replies, in typical British style 'Not bad'. At which the American gets angry. He thinks Peter has insulted not only his cooking, but his generosity.

That's us. That's the British. We're too self-conscious, too reserved.

You work hard don't you? So if you work hard, why don't you get the credit you deserve? And this is how you do it…

553. The STAR system

- Situation
- Task
- Actions
- Result

If you stick to these four headings when you are giving a review of what you have done, you can't go wrong.

Life-shock anyone?

I came out of university thinking I knew it all, and was shocked to find I learnt more about life, people, business, and customers, in the first three months of work, than in three years of study.

I vividly remember talking to a middle aged guy who was maintaining the printing presses (I worked in local newspapers at the time).

Here was I my new work suit, and he was there in his ink stained overalls, complete with oily fingers and dirty face, looking a complete scruff. The contrast between us couldn't have been sharper.

But ten minutes into our conversation I had a revelation. This 'scruffy guy' knew more about the local newsprint industry than I did… or ever would.

I'd had a Life-shock. I'd had a mental kicking I would never forget.

I learnt that if I wanted to succeed, I should learn to listen, and accept that everyone has something to offer, no matter who they are, if you are prepared to hear them out.

554. You have two ears and one mouth, so you should listen twice as much as you talk.

But surely you need an education?

Education is a double edged sword for someone in a marketing role. On the one hand, an education helps you 'see' the world and understand it.

On the other hand, an education helps you 'see' the world and understand it… in the way you were taught to see it.

To start using commonsense marketing you need

A computer, a printer, and access to the Internet (failing this you will need a pen or pencil, and a notepad).

A reasonable – though not necessarily brilliant – standard of English.

An excellent understanding of the product or service you want to sell, and who your audience is.

Here's the last secret:

555. You don't need to know all the theory to be able to create good marketing.

I built this modest book upon the shoulders of giants...

...here they are:

It's not how good you are, it's how good you want to be – Paul Arden; Phaidon.

Whatever you think, think the opposite – Paul Arden; Penguin

Tribes – Seth Godin; Piatkus

Meatball Sundae – Seth Godin; Piatkus

The Long Tail – Chris Anderson; rh business books

The Tipping Point – Malcolm Gladwell; Abacus

Blink – Malcolm Gladwell; Abacus

Outliers – Malcolm Gladwell; Allen Lane

Yes! – Noah J Goldstein, Steve J Martin and Robert B Cialdini

Made to Stick – Chip and Dan Heath

Successful Direct Marketing Methods – Bob Stone

Commonsense Direct Marketing – Drayton Bird

Sales Letters that Sell - Drayton Bird

On Marketing – Ogilvy

Tested Advertising Methods – John Caples

Blood, Tears and Folly – Len Deighton

59 Seconds – Professor Richard Wiseman

The 4-hour Work Week – Timothy Ferriss

Wikinomics – Don Tapscott & Anthony D Williams; Atlantic Books

Ideas – James Webb Young

With grateful thanks for the support…

Linda Ward, Wendy Sullock, David Sullock, Sharon Platt, Paul Crosby, Andy Atkinson, Jo Ray, Guy Donathy; Chris Gott; Michael Barber; Peter Wilson; Jo Lennon; Melanie Dawson; Jim Scott, Melissa Crowther; Tim Leigh.

About the author

Jason D C Sullock is the Customer Marketing Manager for FTSE 100 Company, Sage (UK) Limited, where he leads a team of eight experienced and professional Marketers.

Prior to taking the role at Sage, he managed marketing and telesales teams with the cable TV, telephone and broadband company - ntl, working successively in the Yorkshire region, Teesside, and then promoting new technology to the small business community and the Education sector across the UK.

Jason has also marketed Apple and pre-press products to the print industry; and spent nearly three years developing marketing for a regional newspaper.

He lives on Teesside, in the UK, with his partner Linda.

Photograph by Michael Tulip, March 2010

www.ingramcontent.com/pod-product-compliance
Ingram Content Group UK Ltd.
Pitfield, Milton Keynes, MK11 3LW, UK
UKHW041928190726
13854UKWH00004B/1504

9 781445 700526